Lessons in Grief & Death

Praise for Lessons in Grief and Death

"This book provides excellent, practical suggestions for supporting a person with developmental disabilities who is dealing with grief and loss. A beautiful guide reflecting real life experiences and providing excellent suggestions for supportive counseling."

ANGELA KING

PROGRAM DIRECTOR

VOLUNTEERS OF AMERICA

"Linda's words brought tears to my eyes because of her depth of compassion and her special gift of helping disabled individuals understand grief! Thank you, Linda!"

KELLY A. BALTZELL, M.A.

WWW.BEYONDINDIGO.COM

"A truly compelling pioneering book that will provide a wealth of insights and courage both for professionals as well as those who care for those challenged by developmental disabilities. I cannot recommend it highly enough."

RABBI EARL A. GROLLMAN, DHL; DD

AUTHOR OF LIVING WHEN A LOVED ONE HAS DIED

Lessons in Grief & Death

Supporting People with Developmental Disabilities in the Healing Process

Linda Van Dyke

Forewords by
Orieda Horn Anderson and
Rev. Gary W. Wagner

High Tide Press
Homewood, IL

Published by High Tide Press Inc.
3650 West 183rd Street, Homewood, Illinois 60430

Copyright © 2003 Linda Van Dyke

Van Dyke, Linda, Lessons in grief and death: supporting people
with developmental disabilities in the healing process /
by Linda Van Dyke –1st Ed.

ISBN 1-892696-30-4

Designed by Shelley Webb
Illustrations by Sharon B. Suess

*Names have been changed to protect the privacy of the individuals.
Proceeds from the sale of this book go to help people
with developmental disabilities.*

Printed in the United States of America

First Edition

Dedicated to my Grandpa, who taught
me to love life and respect death

Table of Contents

Foreword

Often, the public's perception of persons with disabilities is one of a straight line on the graph of a brain wave test. We fail to realize that the receptive skills of a person with developmental disabilities are basically one hundred percent. It is the play-back button that does not always function. They are *not* emotionally retarded. They are capable of loving with more depth than most people who are considered "normal." Their emotions are fully intact.

Through her unique talents, Linda uses art, music and drama to bring into focus the cycle of life and the beauty of the final separation of the physical body from the eternal spirit. In this way, she gives an understanding of the infinite nature of God, the supreme being.

Linda Van Dyke is my personal, professional, and spiritual soul mate. We met over a decade ago. Please share with me some of my innermost thoughts of this compassionate, insightful woman as she shares with us her insights and experiences of the cycle of life. *Lessons in Grief and Death* is a powerful book about life and death and the grieving process of saying good night to someone we love.

Catherine Marshall, in her book *A Man Called Peter,* offers these consoling words: "We believe in God. We believe God is everywhere. We believe when our loved one dies, the spirit goes to God. How can they be far from us?" With simple wisdom and vision, Linda brings Marshall's concept into focus by providing a personal point of reference to the precious time before death. With her genuine compassion, she gives credence to the song "All Day, All Night, Angels Watching Over Me." Throughout her teaching of faith, she brings solace to those who are feeling abandoned through death.

Using true stories to capture and illuminate, Linda untangles the complexities that dying and death present. This book is not just for persons with disabilities, but for everyone.

With the heritage from her wonderful, insightful grandfather and her deep faith, Linda is able to share joy, comfort, extraordinary kindness and compassion. She embraces all faiths; thus, she sees the beauty and value of each soul. She has the ability to reach into the interna of those to whom she ministers, touching their hearts. She teaches that tears are the therapeutic bleeding of the heart.

In advocating for persons with disabilities, Linda teaches the rights of this population to grieve in their own way. Their concern is not "what people think." They cut through the "fluff." They have no image, no prestige to live up to. Many are not even notified that a family member has died. Many are not allowed to attend a family member's funeral. Some families fear that their method of expressing grief will not conform to the family's composure, image and/or prestige. This is a form of abandonment that delivers a damaging blow to the person's psyche each time it is revisited through memories. Persons with disabilities "get it." Often, the general public does not.

Charlie Brown always says, "Good grief." Linda teaches how to turn grief into something good by making the spiritual connection.

Linda's teaching personifies the saying, "Death is not extinguishing the flame, but putting out the lamp because the dawn has come."

My sincerest wishes for each person who reads this beautiful book are solace, comfort and a new level of understanding. When death comes and we say good night, all of our wealth will be measured by whom we loved and who loved us.

ORIEDA HORN ANDERSON
DEVELOPMENTAL DISABILITIES CONSULTANT,
EDUCATOR, AND AUTHOR OF
DOING WHAT COMES NATURALLY?

"The major experiences of common life reveal what is in a man as fire reveals what is in the crude ore. They reveal pitilessly either our poverty of spirit or our resources!"

Elton Trueblood

The art of communication with persons with disabilities requires utilizing every possible medium to stimulate the heart and soul to respond to the common experiences of life. It is often said, "persons with developmental disabilities are concrete thinkers and have difficulty with abstract concepts." Therefore, communication about death and dying must utilize all of our senses to comprehend and understand the experience of death and for the meaning of death to transcend the concrete fact to inspire faith and hope.

All too often in our communication with persons with developmental disabilities we rely on the medium of "talk" or "conversation" to deal with a difficult topic without consideration of the "hearer's comprehension." It is easy to assume that when a person with developmental disabilities looks normal, normal communication methods will be effective. When this occurs, the person with disabilities may simply hear a barrage of words, WORDS, WORDS!

A second predicament in which we often find ourselves is failing to listen to the person with disabilities express through words, drawings and or behavior when attempting to cope with one of life's most difficult experiences. To assist a person with disabilities effectively navigate the grieving process, it is paramount that we listen for the full range of emotions and feelings naturally and normally experienced, and then offer meaningful ways to express them.

How I wish that I had received this manuscript just three weeks earlier. The oldest person with developmental disabilities at Rainbow Acres died at the age of eighty-two. As each person expressed his or her sense of loss and celebrated Jules' life, we needed one unifying experience that could symbolize our gratitude and release him to be with God in heaven and enjoy the blessings of eternal life.

Linda Van Dyke takes the everyday balloon and breathes into it new meaning and purpose as a symbol and communication device to empower persons with disabilities to transcend the concreteness of death–their grief–to experience faith, hope and peace!

Throughout her career in ministry with persons with disabilities, Linda Van Dyke has used singing and music, art and drawing, storytelling and drama, photograph displays and slide presentations about the loved one to empower persons with disabilities to celebrate life's common experiences and navigate the grief process. She is also the consummate sensitive listener as the person with disabilities attempts to articulate by word, drawing and behavior the deep emotions they are experiencing. In short, Linda Van Dyke has become a trusted friend and advocate for hundreds of persons with disabilities.

It is out of her ministry with persons with disabilities in the grief process that Linda Van Dyke has tapped into rich resources and developed this series of learning experiences, communication experiences with a simple balloon that empower persons to successfully navigate the grief process and deepen their faith.

May you find these stories and lessons empowering and inspiring spiritual resources for yourself and the persons you serve!

Rev. Gary W. Wagner
President
Rainbow Acres
Camp Verde, Arizona

Introduction

Balloons have always fascinated me. As a child, a balloon was my favorite thing to buy when my grandmother took me shopping at the local dime store. I loved watching them float through the air as if they had wings or feet with which to dance. My children loved balloons, too. They were the first decorations we bought for all the birthday parties over the years. Today, as executive director of Luvability Ministries (a not-for-profit organization that focuses on the development of spirituality in persons with disabilities), I often use balloons for drama productions and in music. They leave a lasting image of good, happy times of celebration.

During my years as a therapist for people with disabilities, I learned that balloons were the keys to releasing painful experiences. People with disabilities often suffer great emotional losses from abandonment, abuse, neglect and isolation. It has always amazed me how people with disabilities can process such human pain, while many of us who are not disabled linger in painful places for years.

The practice of ending the session with the final release of the balloon helps those who participate in the experience find closure in the loss. The therapist who learns and practices the model also experiences closure. All of the stories in this book are true. Each one ended with the rising of a balloon in celebration of the life of the deceased. For some, one balloon was indicative of the letting go. For others, several were sent up. I recently attended the funeral of a young minister who had died tragically. Hundreds of balloons were sent up in his honor. The cold winter day and the brilliance of the snow that was softly falling created a breathtaking view as the colored teal balloons rose to their destination–a destination that is far beyond the person who holds the string and releases the balloon.

My purpose in writing this book is to share with the reader a very practical therapeutic model that is based on a simple balloon. Anyone can teach the model. It is a beautiful experience to be part of the life of one who loved and their acceptance of another person's death.

Helium gives balloons life. The balloons move up and often wiggle their way to the clouds. A pretty-colored ribbon connects the hand to the balloon, only to be let go when inner peace and comfort comes to the heart. The balloon appears to have a purpose when entering the heavens. Metaphorically, the image is healing to all those who suffer loss. Looking up and watching that colored balloon become smaller and smaller as it is welcomed into the sky helps to confirm the loss and helps the one who released it connect to the disappearing.

There is something mystical about spirit–anything with a spirit. The balloon becomes the link between the mystical and the real as it moves to the place that the wind takes it. *Lessons in Grief and Death* is a concrete way to teach people with disabilities about the acceptance of loss. With the letting go of the string, the balloon soaring to its final destination and out of sight, the experience proves to be one of hope and understanding.

In my work, I have seen hundreds of balloons released to the heavens by those with disabilities and those without disabilities. The same reaction is present. Saying goodbye and sending the wishes through a colored balloon brings closure to physical pain and brings peace to the heart. As you begin to release balloons in your own work, may you be comforted in the experience, for in accepting the finality of death, we understand the cycle of life.

Throughout this book, the reader will encounter the word "individual." Language and respectful terminology has been consistent in addressing those with disabilities. Society has moved far away from the verbiage of *retarded, Mongoloid, insane, asylum* and *idiot.* We have, instead, brought respect to the words we use. The blind are now visually impaired, the deaf are no longer hard of hearing, but hearing impaired. Mongoloid has been replaced by the approriate label of the condition, Down syndrome. We have accepted mental illness as a disease that needs constant treatment. Crippled and lame have been replaced by the language of physical disability. It is out of this respect that I choose to identify those who have participated or will participate in the loss model as individuals. To be an individual is to be equal to all people. This language challenges the reader to disconnect the disability from the person. I am an individual. A person with a disability is an individual. You are an individual. All people are individuals.

Part One

Chapter One

Randy's Story

One very hot Indiana day, I arrived at my office and found Linda, my office mate, crying. As the director of a day program for persons with severe and profound cognitive disabilities, Linda was continually seeking ideas and services that would offer new ways to provide "learning" to those for whom learning was difficult. She was an innovative leader who fought the use of childlike games, musical toys and button switches that produce reactions. Instead, she advocated relationships and relational activity. She preached and preached her love for individuals whom society often saw as costly and wasteful.

On this day, she was crying over the report of one person, a man I will call Randy Gronel.

Randy was fifty-one years old. His father died when he was a child. His mother then dedicated herself to raising him alone. They were together in spirit, yet far apart from the realities of life. Mrs. Gronel drove him to a day program in a big car that was very old. It was one of those vehicles that car dealers love to describe–only one owner, not a scratch on it, low miles.

Every day, for more then twenty-five years, Mrs. Gronel dropped off her son at the program. Randy was wheelchair bound. He would move his feet sluggishly across the floor to propel himself in his wheelchair wherever he wanted to go. He was very good at it.

One day, the staff noticed that Randy had not attended the day program for a couple of days. Since it was not unlike his mother to make a quick trip to visit her sister in the nearby state of Michigan, no one at the center was too concerned. But the next week, after four days of no show, the social worker who was assigned to Randy began calling his home. No one answered. She assumed that Randy and his mother were out of town. But, the next week brought more no-show days, so the social worker decided to visit Randy and Mrs. Gronel at home.

The social worker arrived to find Randy in his chair. The report of this home visit was the cause of the director's tears. He was extremely thin, confused, hungry, bearded, dirty and hot. His mother lay dead in her chair. The coroner determined that Mrs. Gronel had died some eight days earlier. Randy had lived on the cereal that his mom kept on a bottom shelf within easy reach for him.

After Linda read the report, she left our office and went to bring Randy to her home. Her husband helped Randy shower and shave. They served him his first hearty meal in many days, then she called me to come over and work with him. As the Human Awareness Consultant for the largest mental health support agency in South Bend, Indiana, I often supported persons with developmental disabilities through the process of grief. The process usually starts with addressing the basic facts. With Randy, I would begin by telling him his mother was dead.

When I arrived at Linda's house after the supper hour, Randy was sorting through a big box of baseball cards. They were in no order. Order would not mean anything to Randy. He fumbled with the cards and dug deep into the box, watching as they rolled over his hands. I looked at his gaunt face and thought about all that boxed cereal and wondered why manu-facturers are allowed to claim that they are full of vitamins and minerals. Perhaps Randy ate from a box that went through the assembly line last and did not get any. His face was different. He was so thin!

I sat down and began to talk to him about his mother. I explained that it was time for her to die and she would not be with him anymore. He would need to find a different place to live, but for this night and a few after this, he would stay with Linda. He did not cry or talk or look at me. He did not respond at all. Instead, he continued scooping up the baseball cards and watch-ing them drop to the bottom of the box.

I promised Randy that I would stay close to him in the next few days. I would do anything I could to facilitate his understand-ing of the experience he had lived for the past two weeks. I have often wondered since that moment why Randy's story triggered such guilt in me. Was it my interpretation of what he must have felt being in the same room with his dead mother? Was it an acceler-ated crossing of professional boundaries in my support for him? Or, was it my anger about overworked social workers who did not check on him in a timely manner? It probably was a combination of all of these feelings and issues. Regardless, they all stem from a clear understanding of the supports Randy needed at the time of his mother's death.

I wished Linda good night. On the drive home, I wondered how my son Danny, who also has a developmental disability, would find out about my death. The thought of a person with disabilities living on cold cereal for weeks tormented my spirit. I silently vowed to teach Danny how to cook.

Before the funeral, I explained to Randy the process of burying a body. I attended the wake with him. Many people there shook his hand, smiled and gave the traditional condolences: "You will be okay now; Mom is in heaven." They walked away, discussing what it must have been like in the apartment, in full hearing range of Randy. I sat in a corner, waiting until all of the visitors had left. I suggested to Randy that he might like to bring something the next day to place in the casket with his mother.

On the day of the funeral, Randy arrived neatly dressed in a shirt and tie. He held a paper bag tightly in his hand. Linda was crying again. She said Randy had dumped all of his baseball cards in the middle of her living room the night before. He had crawled around the pile, picking out some to send to heaven with his mother. In the visitation room, Randy wheeled close to his mother's open casket. He began meticulously lining up the cards he had chosen all around her body. Every one featured a California Angel.

Randy's story, and his angels, made a lasting impression on the people who supported him. They remind us that people involved in the life of a person who has a disability must take the time and make the effort to allow all that is human to surface.

Randy's story is dramatic, but his needs are no different from anyone else's. The needs of an individual at the time of death are simple. It is life. It is the connection with another human being who understands, who comforts, who is present. For at the moment of death, we are reminded of all that makes us human and alive. This basic right was not available to Randy. He faced it alone, as best he knew how.

When helping an individual deal with a traumatic death, the counselor or staff member can explain to the person that death is inevitable. It is the end of the cycle of life as we know it. Dirty clothes complete the cycle in the washing machine. The machine knows exactly when the cycle is finished and shuts off. Completed. We should take lessons from the knowledge that all things eventually come to an end–even life.

Often the washing machine gets stuck in a cycle that cannot be completed on its own. It needs help, adjustment and intervention to finish the work. It is a cycle that does not work without careful attention.

Sharing a traumatic death is never easy. A good coping tool to share with those who are often left as "victims" is to give value to the idea that the person died too soon. We usually think of someone who has died as being old, of bodies getting sick and becoming too tired to breathe anymore. When an accident happens and death comes quickly and early, there is a break in the natural cycle. The washing machine metaphor helps the person with a disability understand that the trauma involved is an unforeseen and untimely loss.

Once the person understands how the loved one died, it is then important for the counselor, teacher, social worker or minister to present the grief work from the cycle of life perspective. They must be patient in addressing the shock that is present when someone dies tragically or too soon.

When helping an individual deal with murder, suicide or accidental death, the truth should never be compromised because of a disability. There is a basic absolute in life and that is truth. We as support staff need to allow for individuals to process truth in their own manner and in their own time. If a murder has occurred in a family, the individual has the right and should be given the opportunity to ask questions and have them answered. Information should not be guarded. Dealing with death by murder or suicide provides the individual the opportunity to recognize their personal values and their own mortality. It can provide strong moral value to life itself. Never should the counselor use the situation to promote his own value system. He should, however, provide the individual with the needed information that reflects death as a part of the process of living. If the process is interrupted by choice, then it is not the natural cycle. Just as the washing machine getting stuck on a cycle is not right, so too is a death by trauma or suicide not right.

Randy's story has a much deeper component than the process he went through when he found his mother dead. Many single mothers in our society are raising children with disabilities. It is a societal issue that more social workers, service providers and support staff need to recognize. The loss of one's mother is a universal awareness of any son or daughter's own mortality. It is the visual recognition of the next generation making their own way.

For a person with a disability, the experience is heightened–especially one whose sole dependence is on a single mother. The counselor should not only be aware of the grief process the individual is experiencing, but should consider supporting the individual through the transition from feeling alone, abandoned or rejected to feeling strong, connected and supported. With this added component, independent growth can occur. In my work with Randy, I was able to empower him to "become the man Mother worked so hard to teach him to be." He was able to comprehend the message and better accept his role as someone who is still alive.

Lessons for Healing after a Sudden Death

When a loved one dies suddenly or unexpectedly, it can be especially difficult for a person with a developmental disability to come to terms with the loss. His initial reaction may range from anger, to shock and disbelief, to serious depression.

As support staff, we must first explain to the individual the truth, that his loved one is really gone. We must also let him know that he will not always feel anger or sadness, and that there are people who can help him get through this difficult time.

Discussion

When helping a person understand a death loss, the following discussion steps are helpful.

1. Reassure the person that he did not do anything to cause the death.
2. Let him know that life can sometimes seem unfair.
3. Explain to him that everyone will die at some time.
4. Explain that the deceased feels no pain.
5. Discuss how, in addition to sadness and anger, he may feel a certain kind of hurt (frightened, cautious, or suspicious) because the loss happened without any warning.
6. The person may feel that since his loved one died without any warning, more bad things will happen. Explain to him that just because we feel like something bad is going to happen, it does not mean it will.
7. Understand that the actual experience may stay in the individual's mind. With your help, he can change how he thinks about it. Explain that when the pictures of the experience come to mind, a good way to help accept the loss and honor the sad feelings inside is to change the pictures. Have him

replace the pictures with good memories of things he did with the deceased before she died. Discuss how pictures of happy times together become memories, and how remembering the person he loved helps him to understand that all kinds of feelings happen when someone dies. Explain that when the pictures in his mind turn to happy times, the feelings begin to change. The word for feeling is "emotion." All people are full of emotion when a loved one dies.

Activities

1. Establish how the news came to the individual and what effect it had and continues to have. To get a very traumatized person to talk or share, assemble picture cards of simple drawings. They should depict people talking, sharing a meal, hugging, listening to music, walking, petting a cat or dog, housework and other common activities. Spread them out on a table or the floor. Allow the person to pick any picture he wants to jump-start a discussion.

2. Invite the person to bring in something that reminds him of the person who died, especially something the deceased gave to him or a photo of them together. Point out that the deceased loved him and the gift or photo shows it.

3. Create a memory box with items that remind the individual of the deceased. Do not rule out items from the kitchen and bathroom that have a special smell (lotion, a bar of soap, a spice or coffee).

4. Have the individual draw pictures. When he is ready, encourage him to draw the deceased looking safe, free of pain, smiling at the individual, and so on.

Chapter Two

Dominic's Story

A social worker called me one day. "I can't stand this anymore," she said, "Valerie's dad is terminal. She has been crying for the full two weeks that he has been in the hospital. She should be over this by now. Her quota is down at the workshop, the group home staff say she is up at night asking for continual drinks of water, and she brings half of her lunch home each day. I may have to provide additional staffing and we cannot afford it. Can't you get her to understand this? I'm exhausted with all the extra documentation I have to do just dealing with her issues. I will be glad when her dad finally dies and I can get some peace."

I have been called in on many cases to teach an individual like Valerie the cycle of life, usually at the end of the cycle. It never ceases to amaze me that we (specialists in the field of developmental disabilities) can spend hours designing special methodologies that teach skills such as brushing one's teeth or cooking a certain type of meal. We document the percentages of success, try every available means of completing the goal, and rewrite it if the progress does not match the outlined criteria. Yet, at the time in life when all that is sacred becomes important–often crucial to the very understanding of independent living itself–we hurry it up. We avoid dealing with the stress of the situation and chart it as "escalating behaviors" instead of facilitating the balloon experience of letting go, accepting, and gaining comprehension of the life cycle. Perhaps if we study and use these techniques to support and teach the grief process, it will present less difficulty to the caseworker than the toothbrushing goal!

Several years into my practice, I talked with my friend Marie about sharing information on the life cycle (including sexual issues) with her son. Teaching Dominic was and still is important to her. She listened and prepared the way for him–or at least she thought she had–until the day her husband Jerry died. On that day, I received a phone call from the local hospital emergency room. Since I happen to live across the street from the hospital, I answered the call and looked out the window at an ambulance parked outside the emergency entrance.

"Hi, it's me," my friend of seven years said. "Jerry is dead. He just died. I'm over here at the hospital."

"What do you mean he died?" I replied. "I thought you went to a wedding." I heard a click and the line went silent.

Across the street, Marie's two eldest daughters were

running into the emergency room. I immediately thought of their younger brother Dominic. Where was he? A twenty-six-year-old man with Down syndrome, Dominic had many health issues connected to his developmental disability. His kidneys, heart, mind and overall physical stamina had been affected. By age thirty-three, his body would be comparable to a man of sixty-six who did not have Down syndrome. He had been in that same emergency room many times. It would have been less surprising had the call been made regarding his life. However, it was not Dominic's time but his father's.

The wedding had been a family one. Jerry had enjoyed dancing and celebrating. At home afterwards, he napped with his three-year-old granddaughter in his arms. Marie heard what she thought was a cough, the calling of her name, and a thud. She raced to the bottom of the stairs and found her husband dead. He had died in a biological freak accident. As the emergency doctor reported, "He coughed and sneezed at the same time. It took his breath, his air. This was a one-in-a-million kind of accident."

No one is ever prepared for trauma. My half-mile drive to Marie's house seemed to take hours. Once inside, I held tight to Marie. We sobbed and said nothing for a few moments. Then I went to see Dominic. He was in his room playing with his Star Wars action figures. It was an everyday experience for this man with a round face, short stubby fingers, thick glasses and a smile that melted the coldest of hearts. It appeared that nothing had changed in his world, and I wondered how he would ever "get it."

Initially, the shock was manifested in childlike comforting from many people. Dominic's disability seemed to encourage pity rather than understanding. For some members of the family, focusing on Dominic allowed for the postponement of their own acceptance. They were dealing with the disability in Dominic's life and not the reality of the pain they were facing. He was the shield, the wall, and the pillow–the place of safety for his family members. But, what about his right to grieve in his own way? These rights cannot be hidden in disability.

On the day of the wake, Dominic met us at the door of the funeral home and quickly took us to the casket. He seemed oblivious to the reality of the experience; he was only interested in showing us all the pretty flowers. Dominic seemed to be the only person aware of the beauty of the flowers. Sadness permeated the room and the people in it. My friend and her daughters were on emotional overload, with tears flowing each time a new person entered the room. Dominic found strength in our visit; he connected. The flowers provided him with a way to share the story.

My heart ached for this family. As a single parent of a mentally retarded son, I knew the struggles that were ahead for Marie. Raising a disabled child alone is an exhausting experience. The supports are never enough, the money designated for general living always has to go to other places to provide specialized "things" for the child, and babysitters are few and far between. With the social life of the parent nearly eliminated, the child with a disability and the single parent can become an island within themselves.

The relationship between mother and child is almost sacred. It is the mother who recognizes the loss more than anyone else. A parent whose child is delayed in all developmental levels of comprehension and achievement finds her mind wandering to those places that "should have been." While all the neighborhood babies are walking by twelve months, her child still needs to be carried at seventeen months. When the first day of kindergarten arrives, the parent and child with a disability stay in the house.

When tuxedos and gowns are being chosen for prom, and college applications are being filled out, their dining room table is filled with Disney coloring books and crayons. Not an unusual sight in a home with children, but what if the child is a teenager? We parents become experts in pushing away the loss of the child we did not get; we compensate by bringing attention to the accomplishments of the one we did get, even if it is coloring in the lines at age seventeen.

I was a master at it and so was my mother! She thought if she bought the fanciest clothes, the best shoes and the finest toys available, disability would be hidden better. After watching the members of Dominic's family, I knew there were a lot of people whose thinking matched my own and my mother's.

Losses come at all times, in all sizes, all shapes and all designs. As the Bible states:

"There is a time for everything,
And a season for every activity under heaven.
A time to be born and a time to die.
A time to plant and a time to uproot.
A time to kill and a time to heal.
A time to weep and a time to laugh.
A time to mourn and a time to dance.
A time to scatter stones and a time to gather them.
A time to embrace and a time to refrain.
A time to search and a time to give up.
A time to keep and a time to throw away.
A time to tear and a time to mend.
A time to be silent and a time to speak.
A time to love and a time to hate.
A time for war and a time for peace..."
–*The Holy Bible*, Ecclesiastes 3: 1-8

Some family members never move from the loss to acceptance of the loss. In the area of disability, guilt comes from unresolved feelings about the loss. Loss that is multiplied through guilt is very present in the nondisabled population.

In my experience of counseling people with disabilities who lose their only parent, it is not the finality of the loss, but the aftereffects of poor planning or no planning whatsoever leave that the deepest emotional scars. Reactions and responses to needs of these individuals should be bathed in compassion. Once the support is available, the individual is able to move forward and work through the grief process.

People providing supports and services should be aware that many parents who choose to give their lives for their disabled child do not think beyond the time when death will part the relationship. Therefore, the "child" is not emotionally equipped to deal with the loss. Patience is the key here! After the loss of her husband, Marie began to put together a plan for her son that will enable him to make a transition into alternate living when she dies.

The next few years were hard for Marie. She had to go on. She had to work outside the home. And though she has been successful in her daily existence, her heart has a big hole. Near the anniversary date of the tragedy, the hole consumes her. Dominic was left to understand in his own way that Daddy was gone. How, with limited and delayed cognitive skills, would Dominic come to understand the process?

His understanding began to show when Marie and Dominic started attending the same church my son and I attend. It was a healthy experience since Danny and Dominic each had a friend to sit with. At the close of the service, it was customary for the minister to offer everyone the option of coming forward for prayer. One Sunday, before the words were even out of the minister's mouth, Dominic proceeded to the front with Danny following close behind.

No one knew what the request was about, but we later learned that the comfort offered by the minister was what Dominic was seeking. He sought a spiritual connection as comfort in his loss. His friend Danny walked in support to the front of the church. It was a very public lesson in friendship. Many viewed this walk to the front of the church as courageous for the two men.

One of the elder gentlemen in the congregation, Mr. Lewis, sensed the need to stand beside these two young men in their quest for support. He asked, "What do you need, Dominic? What can I do to be with you during this sad time? Would you like prayer?" It was Mr. Lewis's responsibility to be the bridge between the needs of the congregation and the Sunday morning message. Music was playing and the minister who had just delivered the message was preparing to close the service.

"I want my Dad back," Dominic quickly replied.

Mr. Lewis leaned back on the pew, appearing overwhelmed at the honesty of the request. He did not know what to say. His response was typical, not because he could not respond in a spiritual leadership role, but because he was seeing the disability first. He needed support in recognizing that the request was from a hurting person who, emotionally, is no different from anyone who responds to an invitation to find peace in a place of love.

I took Dominic's hands in mine and gently said, "That can't happen. Daddy's body has died and he was buried. We can ask God together to help you understand and make some of the hurt go away. And, we can do that today and every day until you learn it."

He nodded. Danny then held Dominic's hand as these two new "church leaders" took their request to the author of "a time to be born and a time to die."

Concrete. Simple. Knowledge. Truth. Dominic was seeking answers–answers that needed to be processed his developmental level of comprehension. He got them. His heart was far beyond his head knowledge. At the conclusion of the experience, both men returned to their places in the congregation. No one in that congregation was the same after that day. It was as if each person were holding a balloon and the release came at the close of the service.

Over the next few months, I guided Dominic through the grief process using the six-session grief model that I designed for persons with disabilities. He seemed to understand it. About a year later, I was driving over a bridge that crosses the river in my town. A park runs alongside it. A young man stood on the bridge with his arms stretched straight up, extending them as far as they could reach.

The scene looked odd until I realized it was Dominic! I parked in a spot provided for river viewers. Down in the water, pink, plastic flowers were moving quickly in the current. Dominic left the bridge and began walking along the path that winds through the park, watching the flowers.

I called out, "Dominic, it's Linda. What are you doing?"

He pointed to the flowers and then upward. "Dad." I paused for a moment and recognized that the flowers were his symbol of acceptance of his father's death.

"Are you saying goodbye to your daddy?" I asked.

His nod verified my clinical assessment.

"Do you want me to take you to your volunteer job so you won't be late?" I asked.

"No. I'm watching the flowers," Dominic said, and he continued on the path slowly until the current took the flowers far out of sight.

I walked back to my car weeping as I realized my young friend had accepted the reality of the death of his father. I drove directly to the school cafeteria where Marie works. Her coworkers gathered around her, and together we cried tears of hope. Dominic understood. Sometimes balloons float.

Later in the week, Marie called me. She had been concerned about where Dominic had found pink, plastic flowers. There were none in their home. "You know where Dominic got those flowers? While walking to work, he passed the cemetery, went in, found them on someone's grave and helped himself to them! Do you think that's okay? What should I do? Should I try to figure out whose grave it was and replace them? Why would he do such a thing?"

I assured her that the family who placed the flowers would be lifted up by the story. Besides, how would we ever find out to whom they belonged? I saw the process as an act of brilliance for Dominic. He came to the acceptance of his father's death the best way he knew how. Sure, it had pieces that some may find strange, but what a powerful message for all of us. He did it from his heart, with the knowledge that came from that church service months before: there is a time to die.

Dominic's story touched my heart as well as my professional awareness. Those who dedicate their life's work to those with developmental disabilities continue their education with each new story.

Dominic's processing of the grief experience reminds us to value our personal connection to the loss. Recognizing that

there is no "standard" reaction of acceptance provides the individual with personal dignity in the process.

Lessons for Healing after the Loss of a Parent

When a parent dies, the loss can be compounded by the fact that the surviving parent must now face the complicated issues other single parents face. However, as with any loss, the person with a developmental disability can learn to cope and gain a healthy acceptance. Counselors and other support staff can also learn as they watch the healing unfold.

Discussion

In order to more effectively help a person grieve and understand the loss of a parent, it may be helpful to first answer the following questions. If possible, a group discussion may help you understand the views of others.

1. Have you ever experienced the loss of a parent? How did you respond? What were your thoughts and feelings at that time? How can you use how you felt during your time of loss to understand and help the person with a developmental disability who is also grieving?

2. What are some negative ways a person can respond if she loses a parent? What do you think are the best ways of dealing with her reaction?

3. If a person with a developmental disability loses one parent while the other parent is still alive, how might she react if:
   - the other parent is in a heavy state of grief?
   - the parents were separated or divorced and now the other parent will assume guardianship?
   - the other parent is not supportive of the individual's needs?

4. What if both parents (or guardians) die at the same time? How might the individual respond? How can you help a person in this situation?

5. If an individual with a developmental disability loses her last surviving parent, how might she react?

6. Sometimes, due to illness, death is expected but the family and loved ones still feel that they were not ready for the loss. As a counselor, how can you help a person with a developmental disability prepare for the loss? After the death occurs, how can you help the person through the grieving process?

Activities

1. Purchase a photo album or scrapbook. Have the person with a disability bring in photos, postcards, or other items that can be affixed to the pages. These items should remind the individual of her parent or guardian.

2. If the parent was buried, plan a trip to the gravesite. Explain to the person the purpose of the tombstone and the comfort they may feel by visiting the site.

3. The individual may wish to help with funeral preparations. Ask her if she is interested in helping pick out a suit or dress for the deceased to wear at the funeral. Other options may include having her help pick flowers for the funeral or finding a good photo for the obituary.

4. It may be interesting and fun to create a family tree. Use a posterboard, large sheet of paper, or even create a mobile. Include the people who are alive and those who have passed away. Explain to the individual that even though certain family members have died they are still part of her family.

Chapter Three

Danny's Story

Do you want to put something in Grandpa's casket to send to heaven with him? How about one of your wrestling figures?" I asked.

"Why would I do that? He's dead and won't be needing them," Danny replied.

My son has a developmental disability and was sixteen years old when my father died of leukemia. Paul H. Cofield was a wonderful man of simplicity, faith and love for his family and salt-of-the-earth values, as he called them. He was very close to my three sons, his only grandchildren.

It was Danny who gave his grandpa the purpose for living beyond the months his doctor diagnosed.

My grandfather once told me, "Understanding skips a generation." Those words came to fruition in the relationship between Danny and his grandpa.

My dad would become a playmate on the floor for Danny. The wrestling figure dolls would engage in spectacular matches and somehow Danny's character always won. When the days became longer for us and shorter for him, I wondered who would become Danny's next wrestling partner. The connection between these two transcended the relationship between Grandfather and grandson and disabled and non-disabled. It was play time! It was creative expression for both men! The wrestler dolls came alive as their rubber bodies were smashed onto the plastic wrestling ring. Some professionals who work in the field of disabilities are adamant about "appropriate choices and age appropriate programs." This experience between two adult men was very appropriate. Language, creative stories, laughter, conversation, and joy was present in the matches. What is more adult than sharing conversation, story, laughter and joy? Many people spend their entire life looking for such qualities in their daily living. And those are non-disabled people! Danny has taught all of us that play is therapeutic.

Each of my sons presented a gift to their grandfather at his funeral. My older son, a gifted guitarist and songwriter, sang at the funeral. He tucked the words into his grandpa's pocket to remain with him forever. My youngest son, a jock who is gifted at hitting, throwing, bouncing and swinging at balls, placed his treasured end-of-the-season Little League home run ball into his grandpa's casket.

These were prized possessions for each boy, yet it took the grandson with mental retardation to remind us all that death requires the making of memories. Giving up the tangibles of importance would not facilitate expedience of those memories. They needed to come with the words "he's dead." Such harsh words for so many to hear.

Danny's experience of placing something in the casket was miles apart from the California Angels baseball cards Randy (Chapter One) sent with his mother. Randy had no warning, no precursor, and no one to tell him the death was imminent. He had faced it alone and without guidance. Danny, on the other hand, faced it with support, teaching, and the gentle caring of others. Yet, for both men the final goodbye was one of acceptance and awareness. Randy needed to give the angels to his mother as a symbol of his letting go. Danny had let go before the death since the talk of death was all around him for three weeks. He was prepared.

When they receive news of a terminal illness, it is important for staff to guide individuals through the process of dying. It is best to allow the gifts of wrestler dolls and baseball cards to be given during the days before the death. It is also good to use the tangibles during the post-counseling. Individuals will often focus on the item as a connecting memory. Guiding someone through making a memory often means the difference between healthy awareness and acceptance of the death and painful years of being "stuck" in the process of loss that has not integrated the "moving on" process.

Experience has taught me when one is a professional and the parent of a child with a disability, the "parenting" often takes on many forms. Such is the case for the relationship between my son Danny and me. Danny continues to teach me as he continues his life journey of learning. It was through the death of his grandfather that the knowledge of the cycle of life became a reality. This knowledge is the gift of understanding life that comes from disability.

With each anniversary date of the death, the reminders of the beauty and joy in the relationship are captured in those with disabilities. The relationship between grandfather and disabled grandson captures life at its fullest. It is the experience of "honor" that lives on.

Creating a Ritual that is Meaningful to the Individual

It is good to help the individual honor and remember the deceased in an active way that is meaningful to him. This can only be accomplished by talking to the individual and encouraging him to share his thoughts.

Discussion

People show that the deceased was very important to them through their actions. There are different types of rituals, or ways to honor the dead. Some are public and fairly predictable. Others are private and unique. There is no perfect time for some memorials. It is okay to come up with a way to remember the deceased months or years later.

The following discussion points may help you choose an appropriate ritual idea to present to an individual with a disability.
1. What are examples of public rituals that we see today?
2. What are examples of private or personal rituals that people use to remember the deceased?

Activities

1. Ask the individual about rituals-daily, weekly, and annual-that he shared with the deceased. Then, ask about things they liked to do together that were not regular, but rather spontaneous, such as a movie they shared, a pet that they both cared for, a time when they really laughed or got sad together. Incorporate these ideas into an activity designed to honor the deceased.
2. Discuss creative, stimulating, calming, safe ways to honor others.

3. View videos or newspaper and magazine articles that show people being honored after death.

4. Suggest to the individual that a designated special place provides a lasting memory. For example, a place on one's dresser or nightstand is a perfect spot to place a symbol of the ritual. Encourage the individual to design the place independently. A calendar can be added, listing the holidays of the coming year that the individual will face without the person. Recognizing the dates and placing the symbol of importance next to the date is visual and very healing. This activity is especially effective when supporting individuals who have autistic tendencies or whose personal learning style must be concrete and scheduled to facilitate comprehension.

Chapter Four

Danny and Alex's Story

T omorrow is the day," the doctor had said. "The baby's head is in position. He will be born within the next twenty-four hours. I'll see you at the hospital. Do you have a name yet?"

Babies give life a special giggle. Even the hardest of hearts are often melted by the smiles of a baby. Babies are alive with love and trust. So, it is natural that many people love babies. People often cross social boundaries of appropriate distance just to touch a baby's hand or wiggle their fingers under the baby's chin. Interactions with babies offer important opportunities for teaching people with disabilities about distance in social settings.

Death is far away from babies–or it should be. It is always difficult to accept the phrase "a time to die" when it refers to a baby. And so it was with Alex. His two older brothers, ages six and seven, had been adopted. The anticipated birth of Alex after years of marriage and no natural conception was a modern day miracle. Friends of the family planned a baby shower for two weeks after his birth. Everyone knew a boy was on the way. After the doctor told the mother that everything was in place for a healthy delivery, everyone expected that they would become a family of "my three sons" before the next day was over.

Hearing that baby Alex was born dead, a person might question the writer of Ecclesiastes. A baby who would have been so loved, so wanted, so cared for, so nurtured, so everything. A baby who, less than twenty-four hours earlier, was moving in his mother's womb, kicking and letting her know that he was very much ready to look in her eyes. The grandparents said that it was one of those things no one understands.

"Why do babies die?" Danny asked me.

At times like this, I feel more comfortable answering the questions of the individuals I serve than those from my son. I told him that some people die young, some people die old and some people die before they are born, like baby Alex. We do not know in advance the exact time or place of anyone's death. We do know that all people die someday. Something went wrong inside where baby Alex was growing in his mommy's womb. Because it was very wrong, Alex died before he lived.

"Today," I told Danny, "We will think of a way to help baby Alex's family deal with the hurt and sadness they feel. Do you understand that?" I really hoped he did, because it was the best answer I could give at the time.

Danny and I went to the florist. He found two very sad-looking teddy bears with matching bow ties. He picked both of them up at the same time, as if he had been led to them. They were the gifts that Alex's older brothers needed to receive from our family. He gave them to me to hold and moved purposefully to another part of the store. He gently picked up a small, glass box trimmed in gold. On the lid was a picture of a very beautiful sleeping baby. Danny said nothing, but placed it in my hands with the bears. Alex's mother later told me that she cut some locks of her baby's hair and placed them into the box to keep forever. The bears became the security for her two other sons. They held them tightly in the days surrounding the funeral.

I did not need a verbal response from Danny. The bears, the little box and no more questions were the answer. Danny perceived the pain of losing Alex before anyone got to cuddle or sing to him. He offered comfort and support. To some people who work with the developmentally disabled, this is amazing. It is also proof that we must continue to lovingly share the truth with people who have disabilities. For Alex, the life ended before it began. For me, the knowledge that I gained from two sad-looking teddy bears and a little glass box is priceless. In Alex's family, balloons became bears.

Danny and Alex's story is the foundation for questioning the death experience. It just does not make sense for babies to die. There is something unnatural about death before life begins. The important component of helping an individual to understand a baby's death is that not all questions have answers. The reality of the teaching must be that "the only thing anyone understands about a baby's death is that we are all so sad." The feelings of sadness come when anyone dies but they are so much stronger when a baby dies because a baby should not die before it is born.

Sometimes things go wrong when someone is born, just like we feel they go wrong when someone dies.

A baby needs time to grow up, learn to walk, learn to talk, go to school, have friends, and learn about being loved and giving love. We can love a baby even when it dies. Love is what helps us all understand.

Helping an Individual Deal with the Death of a Child

Sometimes we forget that death, be it sudden or expected, can occur at any age. The loss of a child can cause grief on an entirely different level. The shock is likely to be greater, and there is often more intense curiosity about the details of the death.

When helping a person with a developmental disability cope with this type of loss, be prepared for questions. The individual may wonder why the child died, how the child's mother feels, or where the child went when he died. If the death was the result of a car crash or other accident, the individual may ask if the child was killed by a specific person, or who was supposed to be caring for the child and why they failed to prevent the tragedy. Many individuals with a developmental disability experience strong feelings of protectiveness, nurturing and responsibility towards people who are younger and more dependent than they are. Others may identify with a young child and have feelings of fear and vulnerability following the loss.

Discussion

Depending on how long you have known the individual, ask questions to get a sense of her understanding of what has occurred and her feelings about the death. Below are a few questions that may aid in your discussion. Be sure to encourage the individual to ask you questions.

1. Do you understand what happens when someone dies?
2. How well did you know the mother? Father? Other family members?
3. Was there ever a time when you helped care for a baby or a child?

4. What makes babies and small children special?

5. How does this loss make you feel?

Activities

1. Make a picture journal out of magazines that depict people at various stages of life. Start with babies. Support the individual in looking for pictures that share what people do in life–employment, family relationships, school, church, sports, or any activity picture. Choose two or three that represent each age category. Discuss how death can occur at any age. End the journal with pictures of sad faces, or place a sad face sticker next to each picture. This exercise is especially effective for those who are not significantly cognitively impaired. It is also an effective teaching skill for those who are nonverbal.

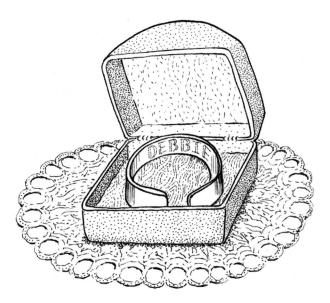

Chapter Five

Debbie's Story

Debbie, you can't throw things like this in the house. It's the third time this week you've thrown things and this time you broke other people's things. What can I do to help you?" I asked the young woman.

"I not know, Linda.... I upset," she said, shaking her head in disbelief. She could not understand that throwing her house-mates' things did not bring the much-needed comfort she was seeking.

Debbie had no family, so she was under a corporate guardian-ship through an agency that protected her trust fund. I met her early in my counseling years. She demanded a lot of my skills, my time and later my heart. In truth, I found myself giving it to her.

Debbie's mother had died of a degenerative nerve disease when she was a teenager. Her father, who died shortly after that, had kept her a child in many ways, all twenty-two years of her life. Then she moved in with her grandmother. For thirteen years, the older woman was everything to Debbie and Debbie was everything to her. Again, understanding had skipped a generation.

When her last relative died at age eighty-three, Debbie was immediately placed in a group home. Within thirty days, she was placed in protective guardianship.

The new home was exciting and, in many ways, it worked for Debbie for about two years. She became part of a very large family that consisted of seven females. But, as the years progressed, so did her awareness of the emotional loneliness she faced daily. Others would go to family dinners, holiday celebrations and weekend visits. With each Friday night, she became more and more aware that no one would be picking her up to share in holiday frivolity. Her celebrations were shared with any staff who could take her home for the day. Presents were never personalized, but were leftover gifts that others did not want or could not use. Gloves must have been a popular give-away; she had a huge collection.

Debbie was never given the instructional knowledge necessary for her to process the reality that the sickness her grandmother was experiencing was terminal. It was her grandmother's wish to protect her from it. This kind of protective support can be very counterproductive. It has caused many individuals added pain that could have been avoided through a process of support counseling and education.

To make matters worse, Debbie had a makeshift bedroom. She was literally housed in a large closet at the end of the upstairs hall. She had many support staff who went in and out the door often. Soon they were ducking as they came in the door because something was usually flying through the room. Debbie was on the end that projected the missiles.

I was called in to help de-escalate Debbie's troubling behaviors. We talked about her grandmother and I sang a song to her since her grandmother was a singer. Even though Debbie had many behavior plans and many behavior plan revisions, none of them had worked. She had pills, psychologist visits, psychiatrist visits and extra staff. Nothing had settled her internal struggles, so she continued to propel things through the air on a daily basis.

After several months, Margaret, the very persistent director of the corporate guardian program, asked me to become Debbie's guardian. "She responds to you and she needs a family," she reasoned.

My very professional response was, "Are you nuts?" Being a single parent of three sons, one of whom was disabled, and taking care of my aging parents did not leave me with much nurture to go around. Despite this awareness, I found myself thinking about it. If I ever became a guardian it would be for a female so the situation would not be too competitive for Danny. I did have an extra bedroom in my house. And, my parents had taught me the joy of service to others. It would be nice for the family of boys to have a "sister."

All of us–the kids, Debbie, Margaret and I–showed up in court all dressed up. I was surprised by the words of the judge. It seemed as if we were adopting her. She would become a part of us. My sons bought her a gold bracelet in a pretty, red velvet box the day she joined us. It was a sweet and tender moment for all of us. Our responsibilities were to stay involved in her life, support her through struggles, provide a welcome at holiday time and remember her birthday. These were simple, human caregiving tasks.

But, our life with Debbie became much more than that. I put frilly, pink curtains in the spare room. I bought a flowery comforter and we welcomed her one weekend a month. It was strange to see frills and bows upstairs among the football pennants, baseball trophies, exercise machines, golf clubs, bats, basketballs and piles of high-top athletic shoes. After five lonely years with no family, she instantly became a sister, a friend, a daughter and a granddaughter the moment she put on that bracelet.

We were her family for nine years. She attended the wedding of her "older sibling," the funerals of her "grandma and grandpa," and she rejoiced in the accomplishments of each member. We rejoiced in her successes, too. I overheard her and my younger son Jacob in the kitchen one day soon after we signed the papers. "Debbie, you better not be throwing anything in this house, 'cause if you do, I'll throw it right back."

Speaking like one teenager to another, she replied, "Not here, Jacob. No way." Together they made the commitment that day to leave things in their permanent place in our home. It worked in her group home, too. About three months into legal guardianship, the calls stopped coming from her home. Things were safe.

I was able to help Debbie understand that her parents and her grandmother did not leave or abandon her. No one had taken the time to teach her about the death experience. Once she processed the loss, she was able to move on, finding strength within herself to accept the aloneness. The struggles and reactions that had come from her lack of understanding were eliminated.

Debbie moved out of the room-closet into her own apartment. She was the first woman in the state of Indiana to have a "therapeutic roommate," a paid support staff person who served as a companion, sharing expenses, supporting Debbie in her weaknesses, and lifting her up in her strengths.

Her self esteem and self awareness grew in the seven years she was part of our family. We talked of her grandmother often and visited the woman's grave. Debbie told us all about her–as much as she could remember and communicate to us. Thus, we gave Debbie a place of memory for this woman who had been so dear to her. We cried with her when she thought of her grandma, but we also taught her about life and a time to die. We helped her to experience love again. When it was time to let go of her grandma, Debbie stood quietly and held tightly to the pink balloon. She looked up and said, "Bye, Grandma. Me love you."

Debbie was able to find employment, ride a bus to her job and earn a paycheck. She often spent her money on gifts for us. We insisted that we did not need all those things, but today the treasures she found at the dollar store have become real treasures to me. She now lives with all the grandparents she lost and the ones she has learned to love in our family.

Debbie's story reminds us of the importance of teaching the life cycle to persons with developmental disabilities before the death of a loved one occurs. Her continual, episodic reactions demanded interaction on many levels. She was substituting her need for human companionship with behaviors that gave her instant relief when she thought about her grandmother. In the bigger scheme of life, the reactions caused her great trauma and complicated the healing process for years.

The important lesson to be learned from Debbie's story is to seek the origin of the behavior. Both disabled and nondisabled people process trauma and unexplained grief through behavior. It is important for the counselor to determine a historical awareness and recognize the timing of events as a result of anyone's death.

People heal from being with other people. Debbie was healed by becoming an accepted member of our family, but more importantly she healed from the inside out. Problem behaviors stopped because she found value in her life, trusted others again, and was able to say goodbye to her grandmother in a healthy way. Debbie's processing and comprehension of her anger and the resolution of those feelings provided peace for her. That peace provided new relationships, self worth, value and family.

Lessons for Dealing with Extreme Reactions as a Result of Loss

Although it is ideal if the life cycle is taught to persons with developmental disabilities before a loss occurs, that is not always the case. As a result, extreme reactions sometimes follow. These may include:
- Violence
- Depression
- Self-destruction (including drinking water excessively, cutting, etc.)
- Addiction
- Promiscuity
- Unexplained aggression towards peers
- Stealing
- Lying
- Psychotic episodes
- Denial (never accepting the loss)

Discussion

Before beginning the counseling process with a person who is expressing an extreme reaction to a loss, gather as much information as possible about the person, his experience, and his reaction.

1. What are some examples of his negative behavior?
2. Is he harming himself?
3. Is he harming others?
4. Discuss the loss with the individual.
5. Encourage the individual to share how he feels when he exhibits destructive behavior.
6. Talk about the good memories the individual has of the deceased.

Activities

1. Invite the person to illustrate his feelings through drawings.

2. Obtain a picture of the deceased. Make several copies. Provide the person with time to hold the picture, and touch the picture. Play classical music to promote a relaxed atmosphere and DO NOT speak.

3. Provide the individual with watercolor paints and a small brush. Painting a picture with simple color is a good release exercise for a person who is nonverbal. Encourage him with statements like, "Look how nicely you put some color on the face of _____. That shows how much you loved her." Allow for the process to be repeated as many times as the individual wants to paint. The pictures can then be stapled together to make a book. Place a sad face on the front of the cover. Provide the individual with sad stickers that can be placed on each watercolor picture.

4. Determine what occupation the deceased practiced. Find pictures of sameness and tell the person's story. For example, "Here, look! These men are doing what Grandpa did before he died. He did good work." For the nonverbal individual, encourage touching the picture. Play music while sharing the story.

Chapter Six

Hurting Times

ASince the beginning of time, society has experienced conflict. It started early, even with Adam and Eve. The apparently simple conflict came between two people over a piece of fruit after meeting a real snake; nevertheless, it broke down the communication, the trust, the relationship, and found the two unable to resolve what had occurred. In our very technical, organized world, the "snake and his apple" can be seen in a variety of ways.

Everyone in America remembers exactly where he or she was when the terrorist attacks of September 11, 2001, occurred.

I happened to be in a class working on a second master's degree. A classmate's wife called him in the middle of a very important teaching moment. The ringing of the cell phone with a very catchy tune interrupted the lesson and the professor was not pleased! The look on the face of my fellow student quickly transcended the moment. He relayed the message. The professor turned on the television and the information became more important than the scheduled curriculum plans. The class was dismissed and I drove home listening to the story on the car radio.

The pictures of those planes hitting the buildings would become forever embedded in my mind as they appeared everywhere I went. Over and over, the images were replayed on television, radio, print media and the Internet. I wondered how those with disabilities were understanding this act of terror. I certainly did not understand it and it appeared that those who were leading our United States of America did not understand it, either.

The pictures of those two towers exploding and the buildings in Washington, D.C., were a constant reminder of the evil snake. There is nothing more scary than a creepy, slithering, hiding snake, one who is mindful of its power and mission. As a child, I once walked though my grandfather's cornfield in southern Indiana. I remember seeing a big, black snake enjoying the warm sun a few yards in front of me. I can still remember the scream. My father came quickly to my aid thinking I had been tragically hurt! He laughed at that experience for years. Little did he know, I was very hurt! The sudden fear of the unknown about that snake shook my very existence. Even my father could not protect me from those feelings I had when I first saw it. I can still remember that feeling of panic.

While living in a rural area a few years ago and building a new house, I saw a snake curled up on the piles of lumber that were waiting to become the foundation for the home. The same panic occurred. It took me years to go into the woods near my new home, for I was assured the snake had a family or at least a few friends. Snakes should never be associated with a beautiful red or green apple that provides such a sweet taste to one's palate. This is surely an example of a contradictory metaphor.

Actions from snakes, or terrorists, appear to be part of our existence these days. People who have disabilities often find a friend in the television set. It becomes the family, the leisure and recreation connection, the socialialization process for those whose experiences are limited, and the "filler of time" when staff have too much paperwork to do. The images of the snake who was piloting those planes were very real to those who watched it over and over. I began to receive calls from agencies whose residents were having trouble sleeping, whose behavioral episodes were escalating, and whose discussions at the dinner table were about planes and fire. There was a need for some special instruction and education for people with disabilities in an environment that would ensure safety and trust. I did not know how to do that, or how to teach safety because my feelings were equal to those who needed help cognitively processing the images. I felt confident that a big airplane was not going to "hit" my small town since there was nothing of significance there. However, I was very aware of snakes and their ability to terrorize.

When recognizing the whole person, one made up of the complexities of mind, body and spirit, we must assume that all parts work together. Therefore, when the evil happenings of war are all around us, we must respect those with disabilities enough to take time to explain. It was the end of a day when feelings were raw, families were torn apart and America was shaken, yet we continued. It was a day when all people reflected on their own mortality and found ways to understand the tragedy. I remember the night of "9/11" very well. For me, it was a day that brought the wholeness of my existence to the core of the experience. My mind did not understand, my body hurt and cried for those who lost their lives, and my spirit needed to connect with those who helped establish the core values I believe in.

My bedroom was completely empty, having just received a new coat of bright yellow paint. The wooden floor creaked as I went into the room that night. I sat on the floor in the empty room and thought of my parents, both deceased, and those three thousand and some who perished. I found myself beginning to sing–first "Amazing Grace," then patriotic songs, then old hymns, then nothing at all. I do not remember how long I sat there in silence, but when I finally left the room it was four hours later than when I went in.

The next morning, as the images were splattered all over the television again, I had a sense of peace within my inner being. I found a personal way to accept the tragedy and deal with the pain. All people have the right to find the answers. We must help and support those who need a little help in finding their own way to accept tragedy and pain. For evil will continue in our world and in our daily lives. "Snakes" are everywhere.

Lessons for Dealing with Tragic Current Events

Addressing current traumatic events should not be avoided when caring for those with disabilities. Often, we allow the media and our own discussions and opinions to become the teaching for the experience. Included in this chapter are some concrete methods of supporting people with disabilities in issues that concern all humanity.

Discussion

People who support individuals with disabilities must be present in so many areas of life for those whom they serve. Try not to discuss your own negative reactions and personal opinions. At all times, respect the environment of another. Personal attitudes and statements regarding war should not be permitted to invade the life of another. Unless the conversation is inclusive, staff-led, and directed with objectives clearly outlined by the goal, levels of conversation regarding the involvement of war should be kept in the proper perspective.

1. Shut the television off and talk! Turning off the television limits the saturation of war pictures and images. People may be more affected by watching war conflict than they can admit or share.

2. Explain to the individual that sometimes we use the word *evil*. It is the opposite of *good*. Ask them if they know the story of the snake and the apple. Offer to talk about the story and share what you know. Inform the individual that there has always been evil in our world. When we are here, together, we feel comforted and safe by knowing it is good to talk. In this

place, we fight evil. We learn to work together to keep the evil out. When everyone is caring about each other and doing our own responsibilities, the good can stay close to us.

The evil that makes war happen belongs to some leaders who have weapons. Soldiers are trying to protect us from such an evil leader. Good and right ways to protect others should always be better than evil.

4. When helping someone develop a core set of values, it is important to allow that person the dignity of maintaining her own values. Teaching universal core values is a good place to begin. A universal value is a thought or idea that is put into action with many people believing in its purpose. A universal value allows those ideals to be baselined and endorsed in all arenas. For example, a universal value could be "children should not be abused" or "animals can be good pets." War can become a universal value by teaching "for most people, war is something to be against." It is of equal value to share the knowledge that "the more we know about war and understand what happens in a war the better we know what to do, and that comforts all of us."

5. Maintain communication and daily routines. It is a time for sensitivity and compassion, specifically for those whose cognitive learning is limited in areas of comprehension.

6. We celebrate life. We mourn death. Losing a family member in combat during war is another example of someone "dying too soon and dying the wrong way." Death should be the focus, and not the cause of death. The death should be faced, and the life should be recognized as one of extreme honor and dignity. Help the individual to understand that "all people have jobs and work to do. Some jobs are very dangerous. A soldier's job is dangerous. Any soldier who

chooses to be in a job that goes to war is aware of the dangers. If someone dies while doing the important job of being a soldier, then we must understand the soldier knew death might occur." This answer to a death caused by the pains of war brings comfort to all, and the words "he gave his life for his country" become a reality.

Activities

1. Share the newspaper pictures. Discuss feelings of fear. Talk about snakes! "What do you know about a snake? Why do you think people are afraid of snakes? Do you think people can act like snakes? Does this picture of war and hurting people make you think there are bad people in our world?"

2. Suggest to the individual, "Let's make a picture together of the good we feel when we are together." This can be a newly created photo album. Provide each person with a disposable camera. Encourage each person to take pictures of the world they live in. Most will take pictures of their living environment, their friends, their social supports and their staff. If family is available, those pictures should be included. The album should be titled "The World I Live in Every Day."

   This activity provides connection to daily scheduling and structure. It is important for each of us to remain consistent in our responsibilities when war and terrorism is happening. Honesty is very important when sharing information about war. Try not to say, "Don't worry." Share the universal concerns about war and emphasize the support, care and protection that you can provide, and do provide, in the regular daily setting.

3. Several key words can be used with acronyms to share concepts and promote maximum understanding. When the second Gulf War began, I was called by three agencies to present an inservice on how to support individuals with developmental disabilities through the constant barrage of images and discussion of war. There seems to be sudden attention to *peace*. Peace needs to be in the lives of those with disabilities whether we are at war or not! However, it is a buzz word for these critical times and should be used in an advantageous way.

Teach the following. It will support individuals in sharing ways they can be peacemakers just where they are.

P ..... Pray.

E ..... Everything is okay when I understand what war means.

A ..... All people want to feel safe.

C ..... Care about others.

E ..... Encourage each other. Everyone is doing the best they can for now.

I put the acronym on a small piece of paper and titled it "A Ticket to Peace." Those participating then placed the card on the middle of a paper that was filled with balloons, The balloons were huddled together at the bottom of the page, with one single balloon rising up to the top of the page. The rising balloon became the symbol of "one who understands" and looks to the higher power, God, or source of spiritual energy that provides peace. It was a most effective lesson. The visual interpretation of "I can help to keep peace in my own world" provided an element of peaceful understanding in the bigger world.

A second acronym that can be taught is CARE.

C .... Create feelings and allow discussion.

A ..... Answer questions.

R ..... Realize repeated images of war can keep us in a place that is scary.

E ..... Encourage regular activity, and identify special ones that bring escape from images and continual exposure to war.

4. A visual tool: "The Colors of Peace"
Purchase a small American flag for each individual. Tie a piece of purple and yellow ribbon to the flag stick. Yellow is the color of unity. Purple is significant in resurrection, new life, and new beginnings. This activity can be completed in a group and music can be used to endorse the concepts. This activity will be especially effective for persons with limited or no verbal skills.

   - When giving each individual a flag, play a patriotic song.
   - When tying the yellow ribbon on the stick, play the song "Tie a Yellow Ribbon 'Round the Old Oak Tree"
   - When tying the purple ribbon on the stick, play "Amazing Grace."

Nothing needs to be vocalized. Let the music and the images do the teaching. Allow the individual to process the exercise and gain comfort and comprehension within the levels of their personal learning styles.

5. Another activity that provides the universal connection is the placing of a variety of coins on the table. Share the words "In God We Trust" and encourage the individual to find the words. Once again, share in discussion and help to establish the connection.

6. Felt banners with symbols or cardboard posters can be designed by a group and placed in the group home or in their workshop. Or, they can be completed independently. Encourage the person to design a poster that shares peace, joy, care for one another, and messages of unity. Refer to the poster when the individual appears troubled by the images of war or expresses anxiety.

Chapter Seven

Linda's Story

A call came at 11:45 p.m. A coworker and I were at my dining room table making party favors when Debbie's roommate Anna called.

"Linda, I took her to the hospital at 4:30. She's had such a bad cold and sore throat, she can't breathe. They are keeping her, and it doesn't look good. They think it might be her heart," she said.

"Is she sleeping now? I can't get there until morning. I can't leave Danny alone," I said.

"I will stay the night, and I'll see you in the morning," Debbie's paid support staff roommate assured me.

When I arrived at nine o'clock the next morning, Debbie looked very pale. She held out her arms toward me and started to cry. I sat on her bed, held her and comforted her as best I could. Outside Debbie's room, the doctor explained to me that they had found a blood clot in her lung and would need to begin medication immediately to prevent it from moving. I went back to Debbie in her bed and asked her if she was afraid.

She said yes, so I pulled her close and began to sing the words of an old folk song: "All day, all night, angels watching over my friend Debbie. All day, all night, angels watching over you." She smiled, nodded and fell stiff into my arms.

I quickly found a nurse. They ushered me out of the room and began moving machines in to monitor what was going on. I looked down the hall and saw Anna returning. I met her halfway and told her it was not looking good. The blood clot had moved to Debbie's brain and the medical team was working on her.

Anna fell to her knees sobbing in the hallway. I leaned down to comfort her and together we came to the acceptance that our Debbie was on her way to heaven.

I called the minister at my church. He knew Debbie well since she had always attended with us when she spent the weekend. It seemed that he had a special place in his heart for Debbie, as his sister, Debbie, has Down syndrome.

"They are putting her on life supports. It looks like she is brain dead," I told him.

"I'll be right there," he said. He arrived with his wife and his three-year-old daughter. The little girl had liked Debbie, and at three, felt comfortable at this end stage of her friendship with the youthful Debbie that she knew.

Debbie remained on life support for three days. I had to make the decision to pull the plug or allow her lifeless body to remain hooked up until the natural process could take over. I talked it over with the boys, the doctor, the minister, Debbie's roommate and the agency CEO. I talked to Margaret (the guardian director), and to other families who had lost children. I talked to God. How could I–not a blood relative, only a paper-certified guardian–possibly make such a decision? Our beloved Debbie, whom we met while she was still hurling lethal weapons, was no longer with us. Together, those who loved her made the decision to let her go. The plug was pulled at noon as I stood over her bed, singing the same angel song.

People came to say goodbye. Margaret was so sweet and gentle with her goodbyes and in comforting me. Jacob leaned over and said, "Bye, sissy." I had never heard him refer to her as that until that day. She was wearing an angel pin. I took it off, put it in my pocket and listened as the minister prayed her into heaven. At 4:40 p.m. she was in the arms of her grandmother and I knew she would not be throwing anything in heaven!

Anna bought a beautiful, pink suit and my sons picked out a pink floral display to match. We planned the funeral to be a celebration of Debbie's life and all she had accomplished. A group of twelve people who minister to the disabled gently pushed her casket down the aisle together. Those twelve people huddled together so that each could place a hand on her casket, creating an unforgettable image.

In her death, she was served, loved and honored. No greater tribute should any person have than the one that was provided for Debbie on that day in February of 1996. More than one hundred people with disabilities, as well as many who were not disabled, attended the church service. Many of her friends were weeping. For me, the event recalled some of my counseling experiences and provided the opportunity to release pent-up emotions. I thought of the losses in the lives of those in attendance who did not have a Margaret to find them a family.

At the close of the service, everyone gathered in the church parking lot. Each person held a white helium balloon as we said goodbye and sang the same song, asking the angels to watch over our friend and loved one. As the balloons released, they divided and went soaring into the sky in many different directions. It was a chilly day in Michigan, with light snow on the ground. However, the sky was a brilliant blue and the sun was shining. We watched those balloons disappear far into the clouds. Debbie would have liked watching them go up. In my heart I knew she was catching them.

We went to the church social hall and shared a wonderful lunch prepared by the ladies of the church. The therapeutic process began at the serving of the ham sandwiches. Together we had facilitated the experience of letting go, and for many, the integration and recovery process was completed that day.

Margaret still encourages me to be a guardian again. The pink curtains are still in the spare bedroom. For us, no one will ever come close to filling the spot that Debbie left empty in our family. I look forward to the day she meets me at the door and says in a very clear voice and a whole sentence, "This is my grandma." And when the balloons rise for me from all those I have learned to love on my journey, I am sure she will help me catch them.

Helping a Staff Person Heal after a Loss

Staff must learn to take time to process their own emotions when dealing with the loss of an individual they have served and supported.

Discussion

When discussing the loss of an individual who has found her way–for whatever reason–into the life of the staff member, the process is emotionally and psychologically deeper. The obvious reality of the physical death is quickly recognized and the staff person is usually caught up in the preparations for the funeral.

It is a good idea to keep the boundaries of professionalism strong and present. It would not be appropriate for a staff person to conduct a group of the individuals' peers for the sake of her own healing. Instead, an appropriate and necessary response is, "Debbie was my close friend. I know she was your friend, too. We both miss her." However, it is also appropriate and necessary for the person providing supports to benefit from a group of staff members who are aware of the intensity of the relationship.

Recalling and describing the qualities that the person with a disability exhibited is a good format for discussion. This provides the staff person with an opportunity to discuss the reasons she was attracted to the person with a disability. And, it allows for a deeper sense of relationship for everyone involved. Personalities, life choices, interests, hobbies, likes and differences are all inherent in relationships. There is no separation because of disability. Exploring this concept promotes great discussions and appropriate interactions between staff members.

Activities

1. Humor! Like others, people with disabilities say funny things. Allow yourself to reflect on those stories and share them with a peer. Write them down and keep them in a place of ritual. For example, one time Debbie put all of her clothes, her two blankets, her two sets of sheets and all the towels in the washer at once. Then she added a whole box of detergent. She could not shut the lid but she attempted to wash them, anyway. The call came from the apartment manager that she had flooded the place. I keep the story in my Bible near the page where Jesus walked on the water.

2. Go to lunch at the favorite restaurant that you and the individual shared. Bring along a staff person who also knew the deceased. Share special memories.

3. If the individual had a job or worked in a sheltered workshop or day program, take treats for the group with an explanation that you are celebrating her life and want to be in the place where she was so happy.

4. When you are alone, write the reasons why the individual was someone you wanted to befriend. What special qualities did she have? What made you go beyond the expected work and become an integral part of her life? Reflect on why you began–and why you continue–your work with those with developmental disabilities. Consider how the person who was special in your life was connected to some of these issues.

5. Buy something special that represents the moments you shared. Keep it as a visual reminder of the closeness in the relationship. All staff can share stories of certain individuals with whom they have had memorable experiences. The stories remain strong and keep most professionals strong in their

employment. Debbie's story reminds us that most human service people are more human than service. They have to be in order to survive the demands of the job. Recognizing and honoring a long-term involvement with an individual who has worked hard to move from stuck places in life is healthy! Once a staff person involves her heart (with appropriate and defined boundaries), the balloon experience at the end of life is validation that people need people. And, people change when they have people.

Chapter Eight

The Senior Group's Story

Rudy was so tall, yet so wobbly. He walked with a cane and an unbalanced gait. He often stopped still, pointed his cane ahead of him and let the world know where he was going. He always wore a cap–he had several–so it seemed fitting that Rudy should take a few to heaven with him.

Rudy was the leader among his peers in a group of seniors. I was called in to teach them relationship skills. It seems almost funny now, teaching people who were all over the age of seventy how to have "appropriate relationships." These individuals had spent many years together before reaching their senior years.

Many of them had lived in institutions because they were born with disabilities in an era when institutional living was mandated the day the baby's footprint was placed on the birth certificate.

Belonging to a group is a basic human need regardless of where you live. During the deinstitutionalization process of the 1970s, many people were returned to their community and found residence in a group home. The new environment and the new opportunities made existence seem more human. As the day program surfaced, many remained a part of the same institutional group, but in a better setting. Thus, the historical relationships of people who had suffered greatly together were bonded in a very special way. They hold on to the memories as they grow old together, understanding the same places of pain, rejection, abandonment and isolation.

In my practice, I have learned to value storytelling. The work is difficult, time consuming and often overwhelming. It is the stories that keep us dedicated. And so it was that the members of Rudy's group were sharing stories on the occasion of their friend Betty's death. They had known each other in the institution and remained connected for years after they moved to the community. It seems that during Betty's many years living in an institution she would often steal cups, matches and magazines. They became her prized possessions. Her friends wanted to send greetings with her in her casket. Her case manager wanted to send a new purse that Betty could "take with her" full of cups, matches, magazines and goodbye thoughts from friends.

I found a picture of Betty and copied it for all of her friends. Many touched the picture of their friend gently. Some held it high and looked upwards. Some folded it and put it in their bags. The visual aid validated their friendship. Looking at her picture reminded them that her presence was very much with the daily group–and had been for years.

Her friend Donald, a roly-poly man with Down syndrome, colored gently on the picture of Betty's face. The exercise was for the entire class. Each person was encouraged to put color on the picture. It was during the exercise that I saw Donald put down the crayon as if to signify color was not enough for his friend.

"What do you want to say to Betty?" I asked.

He put down the crayon, looked up and said, "Tell God hi."

I was instantly reminded of the lonely hours that must have been present in the institutional setting. Life was over for Betty. Donald knew that, and he wished her well. In all those lonely hours together, an intimate understanding of life and death must have been comforting. I have learned that individuals with developmental disabilities recognize that the time spent together as a group is how life and death should happen for all of us.

For Betty and Donald, living together in their early years in a place that seemed to devalue life, they found a way to find worth in existence. It is called friendship. No one should experience death without someone caring about her life. My grandfather once told me to "live your life so that at your funeral every pew will be filled." It is a rare experience for people of Betty's and Donald's age to have the pews filled. Many of their friends have already passed away. However, to have even one good friend is to have walked this earth with joy. I saw that joy in Donald's eyes when he wanted Betty to tell God he was coming later. (Since that time, Donald has also passed away. At each meeting I had with Donald over the years, he wanted to sing "Old McDonald Had a Farm," his favorite. At his memorial, the animal sounds rang out from the pews. We sang it one last time for him.)

It was the spirit of individuality and uniqueness of each person that provided the intimate understanding between life and death. A purse filled with cups and a melodic version of "Old McDonald Had a Farm" are each metaphoric images of a life that was well lived, despite the daily struggles that often occur when disability is present.

Rudy, the senior group's leader, towered over everyone else. He always had a big smile and a curious greeting when I entered his classroom. He always called me by my first and last name together. A handsome man who wore pressed jeans and trendy sweatshirts, usually with a team logo printed on the front, Rudy had many friends. He had grown up on a farm, so he loved animals. He had a skip to his walk that usually led to a conversation about horses. When he became ill, it was talk of the farm that kept him happy and comfortable. When he did not get well, everyone who knew him became prepared for his death. It was imminent.

Rudy's funeral, held at a church, was personalized to bring dignity to all that Rudy had accomplished. When the roommates from his group home arrived, tender care was extended to each of his friends. Bobby, Rudy's good friend of more than twenty years, appeared ready to say goodbye as the van lift lowered to support him. He was dressed up in his suspenders and nice white shirt. No one offered assistance. This task was something Bobby had to do by himself—to be independent, to make it real.

He struggled to move his wheelchair to the casket. When he got very close he reached inside to touch his friend. He smiled, looked at me and said, "I loved him." Bobby laid his head gently on the soft, satin lining of the casket and shed many tears.

Several people shared in the moving experience as the two elderly soul mates ended their journey together.

Lauren, the wife of the church's music minister, sang at the service. She knew Rudy since she often attended the worship service designed for the disabled. Rudy had become one of her favorite people. She liked the bounce of his walk and the fact that he was a gentleman. When he met her, Rudy tipped his hat and then removed it. The gesture was one of respect for her. Lauren often sang at funerals, but on this day singing was not just a part of her job. It was a heartfelt gesture by a woman who had a friend, an old man who had a disability. She gave him the same respect with her beautiful singing voice that he gave her so often when he tipped his baseball cap. The song told a story. She sang about a gray-haired man who loved to sit on a park bench, watching the birds and sharing smiles with anyone who walked by. One day, the man left the park bench forever.

One of Rudy's friends, a man who had limited words, graying hair and a crippled gait, was asked, "Do you know where Rudy is?" The man responded with a look upward, a finger that struggled to reach as high as it would go and a nod. He made a guttural noise that sounded like "yeah." Yeah, he knew!

Rudy's balloons were beautiful. Who knew balloons came in so many colors! When we sent them to the angels to ask for peace and comfort for Rudy, the sky offered the same brilliance we had experienced so many times before. The balloons stayed together and remained in a group until they could no longer be seen. They headed in the direction of Rudy's home, yet there was no wind that day.

We watched in silence until we could not see them anymore. For us, they were gone forever. Just like Rudy–gone, but remembered by those who use wheels for legs, nods for words and balloons on strings for the promise of eternity for all. Those of us who did not use wheelchairs, and could speak and answer questions, learned that day that maybe men who have developmental disabilities and are age seventy and beyond really do not need lessons in "appropriate relationship skills."

Rudy's story reminds us of the beauty of lifelong friendships. Those of us who are service providers, staff, teachers and supporters sometimes forget the humanness that comes from years of being together in the same places, same thoughts, same rooms and same cities at the same ages. The journey of Rudy and the individuals around him who spent those early years together in institutional settings represents a priceless learning opportunity for the next generation.

Rudy's disability took him to places many of us will never understand. His ability to live beyond that history gave his life purpose and respect. He was a good friend to many. In all the painful years of aloneness, he and others whose memory bank is full of institutional pain must find great comfort in belonging to a group and having lifelong friends.

For the person without a disabling condition, working in a classroom or conducting a group in counseling offers a unique, almost mystical, interaction. The synergy that is present in a group of people who have disabling conditions is powerful. The group often creates a "spiritual child"–a union of thoughts, actions, words, gestures and rituals–that are universally understood within the group. Many times, I felt like I had the disability because I was so unlike the people in the group. Cognitively and often physically, the difference was obvious, but in the emotional realm this group of connected, similar people were further ahead in the group than I was.

Professionals who work with the developmentally disabled must develop a keen awareness of the dynamics of a group. The group process promotes learning at its best, and provides human connection and opportunities to build relationships. When a group's usual activities are interrupted by the death of one its members, the regrouping experience brings out the great strength of the group. That strength resides in each individual who remains a part of the group.

Lessons for Helping an Individual Heal After the Loss of a Peer

When a member of a group dies, grieving takes the form of honoring and remembering someone who was close in age or life situation.

Discussion

It is okay to celebrate even as we grieve. Losing a peer can sometimes force us to think about our own mortality. Different people are "called" at different times. It is important for us to explain to an individual that just because a person his age or in his group died does not mean he will die, too. Even though that person was very special, he can make new friends.

Activities

1. Create a "remember journal" together. If the deceased person resided in a group home, a good time to create the journal could be at mealtime. Each person can state a feeling or a memory to be recorded in the journal. Document a statement for each holiday or special activity the group home does together. Put a picture of the deceased on the front cover and place the journal in the home in an easy access place. At the end of one year, the journal can be given to the family, the former roommate or a friend of many years.

2. Have the staff person write an article (long or brief) in the agency newsletter remembering the deceased. This is a good way to share institutional history with younger staff and those who are not aware of previous treatment of those with disabilities.

3. Make a friendship chain for each person. This is especially effective for nonverbal and lower functioning persons. When a new person moves into the home, or a new friend surfaces, add a new circle to the chain. After a few months, the circle with the name of the deceased person can be removed and glued on a piece of paper. Balloons can be drawn around the piece that was previously attached to the chain.

4. Choose a song that was a favorite of the deceased. While the group is engaged in activity, play the song and say, "We are going to listen to _____'s favorite song. It helps us to think of him while we are together. He would like what we are doing now."

Chapter Nine

The Day Program's Story

Mary's crippled fingers moved page after page of each magazine she touched, looking for the picture she wanted. The picture was imbedded in her mind, yet we could not figure it out. Then she found it, touched it, and made a sound that proclaimed the picture was the right one. I was speechless. Mary's careful search made me suddenly aware that this woman who visually represented disability to the world was very much in tune with her own feelings, her heart, and the loss of her friend.

The "students" in the class were all over age sixty. The setting was a large day program that provided life skills to persons with disabilities.

The seniors classroom was located at the back of the building. Their needs were easily facilitated there. The bathrooms, the laundry room, the exit door, and the outside patio provided life at its best for most sixty- to seventy-year-olds.

For twelve years, a teacher named Ralph taught life skills in this classroom. These skills went beyond the curriculum pages. He had supported his students many times through the death of a classmate. He found ways to connect with their memories. He did not follow a concrete model of teaching, but his ability to relate to people through pictures, music, stories and sign language was phenomenal. Ralph's age matched those of his "students" and he was a good friend to many.

Ralph was known to take many breaks during the day, often sneaking out the back door near the classroom. He was quick to tell all who knew him that he smoked too much, and, with a funny little grin, "I will quit this one day."

The individuals in his class responded with nods; they appeared to understand the health risk. He found it important to share information about the risks of smoking with them, but found the change in his own life impossible.

As a systematic teacher who followed rituals, Ralph went out of his way to make sure that each of his students who passed away was remembered. The day usually started with music from "The Lawrence Welk Show," servings of a favorite food and decorations placed around the room to honor the deceased. A picture of the person would sit on Ralph's desk. The chair that was now empty was given a special place in the room and covered with flowers. Most of Ralph's students did not talk. He talked for them and memories were made. The student's life was not forgotten; this was only one of the ways that Ralph taught life's lessons well.

Ralph had attended his beloved seniors day program as long as he could physically tolerate the demands of the job. Then he continued when the demands were beyond his capabilities. His needs became synonymous with those of his students. Then one day it was over and he was gone. Ralph's family did not want a traditional funeral, so there was no viewing of the body, no funeral, and no formal way to say goodbye. The grieving for the teacher was constant. The seniors needed some form of closure and acceptance, so I suggested a service on the lawn outside the classroom window.

The men and women planned the celebration of his life. The verbal ones were quick to tell of their teacher's love for pumpkin pie. It had become a party favorite for all, often displacing the traditional chocolate birthday cake. The celebration would include music, pumpkin pie with lots of whipped cream and balloons. The balloons would carry attached notes to make sure he knew just how much his presence would be missed in the classroom.

His daughters were invited to the celebration of life along with the staff from the agency. Many people arrived to find the room filled with balloons that would serve to provide closure at the end of our recognition process.

Mary's expression of grief was uniquely hers. Her search through magazine after magazine was aimed at a picture she had apparently seen already. Finally she found it–a cigarette pack with a circle and a line drawn across it. The inscription read, "Cigarette smoking may be hazardous to your health." Mary ripped it out and gestured to me to get her balloon. She communicated with me in simple sign, gestures and sounds as I tied the balloon to the table. Together we attached the picture to the string.

When I asked if she wanted a message included with the picture, she was very clear about what she wanted him to know. Her message was, "Don't smoke in heaven." Mary used to shake her finger at Ralph every time he lit up a cigarette. They would both laugh and continue with the same ritual day after day. Now Mary could no longer shake her finger at him, so she sent a picture instead.

Her balloon was the last one to rise. The others were well out of sight and hers lingered close to the ground for quite some time. She lifted her hand and waved goodbye as it soared to the heavens. Ralph's story teaches us about learning. All classroom instructors are cognizant of the lessons planned for the day, but there is also a deeper type of learning that can occur. The relationship between teacher and student is a sacred one. For the classroom of students ages sixty and over, the lessons were learned in the heart.

Lessons for Helping a Group Heal after a Loss

Individuals with developmental disabilities need to grieve the loss of staff who pass away, just as they would a family member or friend. As with any close relationship, the individual will have a unique set of memories and feelings to honor, as well as wishes for the soul of the deceased.

Discussion

It will be most helpful to talk to the group as a whole. Talk about what the loss will mean to the group. Discuss how different people react differently to loss, so we should try to respect another person's thoughts and feelings. If the person who died is a staff person or other person outside the group, discuss how someone else will replace her in that role, but will not replace her personality or her place in the individuals' hearts.

Activities

1. Brainstorm, to the extent that the individuals are able, ways to celebrate the person's life. Discuss daily, weekly or annual rituals. Discuss the likes and dislikes of the deceased. Plan together a lasting memorial, a one-time celebration, or both.

2. Make a bulletin board of pictures sharing the staff person's work. Involve the group and place the board just outside a classroom, or in a highly visible location in the building. Invite other classes and instructors to a "We Remember _____ Day." Have a party and share a favorite activity of the teacher. A dance is a wonderful idea, and great fun!

Part Two

Effective Techniques for Grief Counseling

The following techniques for grief counseling can be used as general guidelines to follow while completing the six sessions of the Van Dyke Model for Grief Counseling (see page 101). The staff member providing the counseling should be familiar with the language, body placement, and appropriate levels of professionalism needed to effectively communicate during counseling sessions.

- Provide a comfortable chair for the person receiving the counseling.
- Sit directly across from the person.
- Maintain direct and good eye contact.
- Establish the reason for the session using the following questions.
  "Do you know why we are meeting?"
  "Can you tell me about the sadness you are feeling?"
  "I would like to learn about the life that is over."
  "Would you like to share it?"
- Do not encourage the individual through the process. Allow for emotionality and do not dismiss the release or place boundaries on it.
- Provide tissues in the office or meeting room.
- Play classical music in the background. The music should have no words.
- Do not hug, kiss or patronize the individual during the session. At the end of a session, it is sometimes appropriate to offer a hug, a simple touch on the shoulder, or a gentle holding of the hands to reinforce the counselor's genuine support. To avoid manipulation and dependence,

staff should keep a clear perspective of their involvement. Supporting an individual through a personal loss is part of one's employment and should be recognized as such. Compassion and sensitivity should always be the major support offered.

- Familiarize yourself with the experiences the individual shared with the deceased. This can be done before or during the sessions. Discuss these interactions openly and often in each session. This will foster communication and provide a consistent comfort level at each meeting.

- At all times, maintain the understanding of the finality of death. Share the news as it is. Be concrete. Feel comfortable using the words *dead, died, death, gone, no more, buried, funeral, casket, buried in the ground, tombstone, cemetery,* and so on.

- Discourage family members, staff members, friends or other persons with mental retardation from using the phrases "he's sleeping, "she is going away for a while," or "he has to leave for a while." These statements deprive the individual of the right to grieve the loss and accept the truth. At the very least, they are confusing, even when used metaphorically.

- Allow yourself to become a servant of knowledge to the individual. Share information that balances a gentleness of spirit with a firmness that promotes acceptance. Most professionals use the phrase "people I serve" when referring to their work with the disabled. This is not meant to establish a hierarchy or authoritarian approach. It simply demands a level of servanthood that prevents the staff person from becoming controlling and overpowering.

- Keep documentation of each session. Refer to your notes before each session. Discuss the deceased by name and by her identifying relationship in each session.
- If someone expresses thoughts of dying, joining with the deceased, or suicide in any session, take all statements seriously and report them to the receiving agency.
- At all times, it is essential to recognize your ability and the manner in which you conduct the sessions. Many persons with mental retardation and other developmental disabilities have been plagued by the issue of loss and grief for many years. Apply the knowledge that you processed while studying disability in perfect balance with the model of serving, and success will happen! The individual will gain independence and coping skills.

Once the sessions are completed and the balloon begins to rise, the reality of the death experience becomes a natural part of the life cycle.

The Van Dyke Model
for Grief Counseling
for Persons with
Developmental Disabilities

The following pages contain six one-hour sessions that promote understanding, processing, acceptance and healing in the grief cycle. The methods are concrete and expressive. Therapists, ministers, social workers, teachers, parents and students can apply them to any counseling session. Each session is artistic in origin. Each one provides the individual with a disability with comfort and hands-on opportunities to identify and gain developmental comprehension of the grieving experience. The minimum number of sessions is six; however, some individuals may need eight.

Session 1 - Establishing a Comfort Zone

Working through the grief process is about peace. The first session will usually find the individual nervous and uneasy. The loss is relatively new and very real. It is important for the individual to feel comforted and peaceful. The counselor will provide a peaceful and trusting environment by carrying out the following steps.

I. *Establishing a comfort zone*

   A. Determine the person's likes and dislikes for the purpose of discussion. This initial interaction allows for the counselor to establish rapport and gain information about the individual. It is good to keep notes and a mental picture of these things. Discussing the likes and dislikes with the individual also provides an initial transfer of focus from the loss to the discussion preceding the loss. It sets the scenario for the counseling experience.

   B. Establish a relational association with the person who is dying or who has died. For example: "The person who died was your father. That means he was your mother's husband." Lead the individual into revealing the other relationships that suffered the loss. This approach sup ports the individual in the knowledge that others share the same feelings.

   C. Play classical music in the background.

   D. Discuss the purpose of the sessions. For example: "We'll try to help your feelings of being sad and of being mad. And, we'll see how we can understand together how much the life of _____ meant to you."

II. *Visual perception exercises*

Seeing it makes it more real. Most people process very well what they can see. It is important to provide an opportunity for personal expression. This allows the individual additional means of accepting the loss.

A.   Have the individual draw a picture of the deceased person.

B.   Have the individual write the name of the deceased person.

C.   Have the individual hold the picture or the name and play a song. Songs with the word "remember" in them are recommended.

D.   Allow for emotional disclosure. If the individual begins to display aggressive behaviors during the session, hold your hands gently upright in front of him. Respond with the four levels of encouragement often used in times of behavioral challenges.

> "I know this is hard for you."
> "I am here to help you."
> "Together we will understand."
> "When you are ready...."

E.   End the session with the individual calm and ready to return to the daily environment. Allow for the processing of the first session. The closure of the first session is important for the readiness of the second. At the beginning of the second session, you will review the material from the first. It will give you a clear indication of whether the individual is ready to move forward in the process. Review, reflect and reward. He should be validated for his willingness to move forward.

Session 2 - Why Did This Happen to Me?

This session helps the individual to disassociate the loss from the assumption that it happened to him personally. It gives value to the life of the departed and teaches the awareness that the death of a loved one does not happen to punish anyone.

I. *Discussing death: what it means, why it happens, where the person went*

   A. Respect the values of the individual. If Christian spirituality is present, read the text in Ecclesiastes. Discuss "a time." Relate time lines of memories that are important to the individual. Many readings that offer comfort are available at bookstores, libraries and houses of worship. Poems that share the beauty of nature, relationship affiliation or the gentleness of animals are also appropriate. It is possible to begin a discussion of the seasons, comparing the seed that is planted to the cycle of life. Pictures of seeds in all four seasons help the individual to understand the concept of a life cycle.

   B. Discuss sickness and injury. If the deceased was ill, use the words "sick body."

II. *Visual exercise*

   A. Have the individual draw a body and put black dots or lines in the drawing symbolizing a terminal illness. If an accidental death, suicide or homicide occurred, the structure of the sessions is still appropriate; however, allow the individual to state her understanding of the causes. Details of a traumatic death need to be guarded.

Questions should be answered, but the cause of death should not compromise the completion of the six to eight sessions. It is important to appreciate the feelings of all who would be affected by a traumatic death. Others (family members, especially) can be invited to the sessions for added support and understanding.

B.   Help the individual to feel comfort in verbalizing words related to death and loss. The words *dead, gone, death,* and *over* should be used often. It is part of the healing process for the individual to be able to verbalize ideas like "my dad died."

C.   Teach the separation of body and spirit. (I have yet to experience anyone refusing to eat the inside of the peanut. If the individual refuses to participate in this part of the exercise, simply separate the meat of the peanut from the shell and place them far apart. The purpose is to teach the significance of separation.)

1. Show the individual a peanut in the shell. (Make sure the end has a small crack in it.)

2. Compare the peanut to "the body." Explain that the shell is the part that "holds" the spirit, or the inside.

3. Crack the peanut open. Explain that the shell represents the body that was sick and is no longer needed.

4. Take the peanut meat out of the shell. Have the individual eat the peanut. Explain how "the spirit of _____ will always be with you, never leaving. It becomes a memory."

5. Have the individual touch her own body. Discuss how "that is your body. It is the house for who you are.

It carries your mind, your heart, and the part that everyone knows as you. That inside part is called the spirit. The body and the spirit are not the same."

6. Identify the individual's personal value system. Ask the question, "Where do you believe _____'s spirit is now that the body has died?" Most will reply with an answer that has a religious interpretation, such as *up, heaven, God, Jesus* or will point upward or look upward. Do not impose your own values on the individual. It is important to allow the individual her own processing of her beliefs about death.

Session 3 - Understanding the Finality of Death

This session is very important for the emotional healing part of the death experience. Through the very concrete steps of teaching the preparation of the body, individuals can feel safety and recognize the separation between body and spirit.

I. *Understanding the finality of death and the care of the body*
    A.   Have the peanut shell on the table or desk. Reflect on the experience of Session 2.
    B.   Visual exercise
        Materials
        - a checkbook box with a lid
        - a few sheets of tissue paper in assorted colors
        Process
        The individual gently takes the shell and wraps it in a piece of colored tissue paper. Try to have the individual choose the color. Compare the experience to the preparation of the body. (In some cases, I have helped individuals "bury" the box in a basket of dirt to make the explanation of burial more concrete.)
    C.   Discussing the safety of the body
        1.   "This is a way to keep the body of _____ safe."
        2.   "This is a way for us to know _____ no longer needs her body. We are taking care of it by burying it."
        3.   Remind the individual of the body and spirit separation.
    D.   Burying the body
        1.   Get pictures of caskets from your local funeral director. (They are usually very willing to give

them out.) Place them in plastic covers in a binder or notebook. Allow the individual to touch them, turn the pages, ask questions and process.

2. Ask the florist for pictures of funeral sprays. Focus on the ribbons that state the relationship to the deceased. Relate them to the individual.

3. Ask the funeral director for pictures of a hearse. Discuss the funeral process with the individual. Explain the safety of the body in the hearse.

4. Discuss a funeral home. If possible, make a visit before the funeral and meet the director. If a visit is not possible, ask for a funeral directors magazine. Usually, you will find a visual representation in the magazine. Explain that "this is a picture of the man who will get _____'s body ready for us to say goodbye."

5. Ask the funeral home for flowers and ribbon bows left over from a previous funeral. Allow the individual to "make a bouquet" to keep for his room or group home. This is especially effective for females. They love the ribbons! Allow the individual to leave the session with the flowers.

Session 4 - Identifying Memories

This session allows the individual to process the finality of the experience and begin to recognize the importance of remembering. Once the individual begins remembering and is provided the opportunity to reflect, the process becomes very healthy and is the beginning of the acceptance. The counselor should be aware that this sometimes requires an additional session, and should recognize when more time is needed.

I. *Helping the individual to identify memories*
   A. Explain that "remembering helps our hurts."
   B. Visual arts expression exercise
      Materials
      - an 8.5-inch by 11-inch piece of white watercolor paper
      - masking tape
      - colored ink markers
      - matte frame for picture
      Process
      Give the individual a long piece of masking tape. The tape should be torn in pieces and placed on the paper in any form. A shaped design is not necessary. Play soft music as the individual completes the exercise. After the pieces are on the paper, the individual can color (using a variety of colors) over the entire paper (including the tape). When the paper is filled with color, gently remove the tape. There will be a permanent white "mark" amidst the color in the design.
   B. Discuss the deceased person's lasting effect on the individual. The white design represents the life of the person

who has died. Explain how the mark will never leave the individual's life. It is the life that is to continue. And, all of the colors represent good things to come. The individual can then frame the picture and date it. This exercise provides a wonderful opportunity to tran sition the sessions into a discussion of memories and a reflection on the relationship.

C.   Identify the individual's emotions and discuss feelings related to the individual's memories.

Session 5 - Celebrating the Life of the Deceased

This session provides the individual with an opportunity to celebrate the life of the loved one. Celebrating is the beginning of integrating the loss into the individual's life. It empowers the individual to discuss the loss with an emotional comfort.

I. *Learning to celebrate again*
  A. Start by discussing how celebrating "helps our hearts."
  B. Provide experiences that move the individual toward closure and acceptance.
      1. Share a piece of angel food cake, symbolic of the protection of the angels. Discuss and process.
      2. Provide golden bells for the individual to ring, symbolic of the sounds of the angels. Discuss and process.
      3. Have the individual color a picture of an angel. Discuss and process.
  C. Discuss current recovery and integration with the individual.
      "How are you sleeping?"
      "Is it getting better for you?"
      "Let's share some good memories today."
      "What are you doing these days that would make _____ very happy?"
      "Let's write down some words that describe how you are feeling, what you are thinking about, and talk about how things are different from when you first came in."
  D. Help the individual to understand what to expect of the grief process in the future. Provide a one-year calendar.

Identify the holidays, special days and anniversary of the death date. "Walk" the individual through the year and reflect on a memory of each special day. Support the individual in understanding that a full year without the person must be lived before full recovery will occur. The calendar will provide a connection after the sessions have been completed.

Session 6 - Closure: Here Comes the Balloon

This session is the final and most important in the series. At the center is a message of love coming from the balloon. The balloon release signifies the individual's connection to the deceased. It becomes a sacred moment for the one who is letting go.

The releasing of the balloon provides the understanding of closure on many levels. First, it helps with the acceptance of the death. The note attached is the individual's way of saying good-bye. It also signals the closure of the sessions. Finally, with the recognition that the relationship with the deceased has ended, there is acceptance that changes will occur. It is a very powerful, beautiful experience. After supporting an individual through the process of accepting the loss, and sharing the experience of watching the balloon soar into the heavens, the expression "life goes on" becomes very real.

I. *Releasing the balloon and moving towards acceptance*
    A. Planning a time and place
        1.   Discuss with the individual where she would like to release the balloon. People have released them in many different places–the cemetery, outside the front door of the residence, outside the counselor's office window, or another place of the individual's choice. The place is not as important as the time. It should occur at the end of the sixth or final session.
    B.   Sending a message
        1.   Have the individual write a note, color an angel or draw a picture. Any personal expression is

appropriate.

2. Provide a balloon already filled with helium.

3. Attach the note to the balloon.

4. Release the balloon.

C. Discussing and processing the experience

1. Play appropriate music such as "All Day, All Night, Angels Watching Over Me."

2. Allow for a release of emotions, both positive and negative.

3. Invite the individual to imagine what good things the future may hold.

Appendix A

Living with the Death Experience: Useful Words for Teaching Adults with Developmental Disabilities

1. Say, "I know that _____ died." Do not try to be strong and brave all the time. It is good to cry. Crying is a sign to the world that you understand and your heart hurts.

2. Talk about _____ (the deceased). It is okay to talk as much as you want about your feelings. We call that sorrow. Sorrow is very hard to stop. It takes a long time.

3. Continue to follow your schedule. It's good to go to work, go to activities and do things that make your mind stay busy.

4. Eat good food. Sometimes we get so upset that food does not taste good. Your body needs healthy food while your heart is healing.

5. Exercise your body. When you exercise your body, you have more energy during the day and you sleep better at night. Sleeping helps heal the part inside that hurts so much because _____ has died.

6. Learn the story of "why." It will not make you feel any better to only ask "why" _____ died. Everyone has a

die day, just like a birthday. No one's body lives forever. Can we discuss some other people you know who died?

7. Help others. When you can help another person do something that is hard for him, you will feel better.

8. Draw a picture anytime you would like to think about _____. You can even keep a picture book that holds the stories of your favorite things to do with _____. Keeping the pictures can be called a memory.

Appendix B

The Life Cycle

During my years as a human sexuality consultant, I have taught people with disabilities about life-the cycle as we know it, birth to death. All the space in the middle often proved problematic, even to the most secure human beings. The beginning of life is sweet and accepted. Most people love babies and are attracted to their innocence and dependence. The end of life is holy and sacred. Most people reflect and find the time of death a celebration of all the "stuff" that happened in the middle, the time between the sweet baby and the pain of the end.

Human life is a cycle of growing, learning, relating and formulating thoughts and ideals for the thing we call "journey." On our journey we continually gather information and develop beliefs and attitudes to guide us. The cycle of life is about developing personal values in relationships, intimacy, and identity.

We must present life as it is. We must be concrete, factual and respectful. We must allow for the understanding that one's journey involves history, environment, culture and the right to choices. It is because of this learning that all people come to look at the end of the journey. We respond with statements such as "his/her life is over," "what a good life," "what good stories," "what good memories" and so on. Then, we are reminded through our connection with birth and death that the cycle repeats itself in each generation.

A simple way to teach the life cycle is to meet people where they are in their understanding. I have taught life cycle units to hundreds of people who have developmental disabilities. Including a unit on death and dying education makes the cycle complete.

Suggested Readings

Publications

Childs-Gowell, Elaine. *Good Grief Rituals: Tools for Healing: A Healing Companion.* Barrytown, New York: Station Hill Press. 1992.

Grollman, Earl A. *Living When a Loved One Has Died.* Kansas City, Kan.: Beacon Hill Press. 1995.

Luchterhand, Charlene and Murphy, Nancy E. *Helping Adults with Mental Retardation Grieve a Death Loss.* Philadelphia, Pa.: Accelerated Development. 1998.

Worden, J. William. *Grief Counseling and Grief Therapy: A Handbook for the Mental Health Practitioner.* New York: Springer Publishing Company. 1982.

Viorst, Judith. *Necessary Losses: The Loves, Illusions, Dependencies and Impossible Expectations that All of Us Have to Give Up in Order to Grow*. New York: Simon and Schuster. 1986.

Web Sites
Last Chapters, www.lastchapters.org

GriefNet, Inc., www.griefnet.org

Association for Death Education and Counseling, www.adec.org

Beyond Indigo®, Kelasan, Inc., www.beyondindigo.com

About the Author

Linda Van Dyke has worked in the field of developmental disabilities for more than thirty years. She has a bachelor of science degree in management and a master's degree in ministry from Bethel College in Mishawaka, Indiana. She is currently working on a second master's degree in theological studies.

Ms. Van Dyke has been a consultant, therapist and teacher of very special arts for the handicapped artist. She is the mother of three sons, including one who has a developmental disability. Both of her daughters-in-law teach special education. She informed her sons early on that it was "family criteria" to respect and care for those with disabilities. She is grandmother to baby Jacob, who brings great joy to her life.

Ms. Van Dyke began counseling in the area of death and dying while developing a life cycle curriculum to help people with disabilities understand problematic issues. She has presented the methods she designed for *Lessons in Grief and Death* to many agencies across the United States. She states, "With each balloon that soars upwards that I have been blessed to watch, I am reminded how precious the gift of living is to all of us. May the joy of knowing life at its fullest be revealed to you as you watch the balloons vanish into small, colorful spots in the heavens... and then disappear."